The Giant Book of Prolific Facts

by
Jake Jacobs

* * * * *

Published by Jake Jacobs

The Giant Book of Prolific Facts
Copyright© 2023 by Jake Jacobs

1.

The impala (Aepyceros melampus) is a medium-sized antelope species native to Africa.

2.

Impalas are known for their distinctive reddish-brown coat and unique black stripes on their hindquarters.

3.

They are widely distributed across savannas, grasslands, and woodlands in sub-Saharan Africa.

4.

Impalas are herbivores, primarily feeding on grass, leaves, and other plant materials.

5.

These antelopes are well-adapted for running, capable of reaching speeds up to 60 miles per hour (96 km/h) to escape predators.

6.

Impalas have a leaping or "pronking" behavior, where they jump with all four legs off the ground to confuse predators.

7.

Male impalas, known as rams, have lyre-shaped horns that can grow up to 36 inches (91 cm) long.

8.

Female impalas, called ewes, lack horns and are generally smaller than males.

9.

Impalas exhibit sexual dimorphism, where males are larger and more robust than females.

10.

These antelopes have a highly developed system of scent-marking, using glands on their feet to leave scent trails as they walk.

11.

Impalas have a keen sense of smell, which helps them detect predators and find food.

12.

They are social animals and often form mixed-sex herds ranging from a few individuals to hundreds.

13.

Impalas are known for their synchronized rutting behavior, where males gather and compete for access to females.

14.

During the rutting season, males engage in territorial displays, vocalizations, and fights to establish dominance.

15.

The gestation period for impalas is around six to seven months, after which a single calf is typically born.

16.

Newborn impalas have a distinctive reddish-brown coloration, which helps them blend in with their environment.

17.

Impalas exhibit a phenomenon known as delayed implantation, where the fertilized egg doesn't immediately attach to the uterine wall.

18.

This allows impalas to time the birth of their calves to coincide with favorable environmental conditions.

19.

The population of impalas is stable and widespread due to their adaptability to various habitats.

20.

They are an important prey species for large carnivores like lions, leopards, and wild dogs.

21.

Impalas' alarm calls, often described as a "barking" sound, alert other animals to the presence of predators.

22.

Their sharp senses and vigilance help them evade predation in their natural environment.

23.

Impalas play a crucial role in maintaining the balance of ecosystems by controlling plant growth through herbivory.

24.

Humans have historically hunted impalas for their meat and hides.

25.

They are also a popular subject for wildlife photographers and ecotourists due to their striking appearance and behavior.

26.

Impalas' adaptability to various habitats makes them resilient in the face of changing environmental conditions.

27.

Conservation efforts are important to ensure the long-term survival of impala populations.

28.

They are classified as "Least Concern" on the IUCN Red List of Threatened Species.

29.

Impalas have a complex digestive system that enables them to extract nutrients from tough plant material.

30.

They are known to engage in a behavior called "coprophagy," where they consume their own feces to aid digestion.

31.

Impalas have a mutualistic relationship with oxpecker birds, which feed on ticks and parasites found on their bodies.

32.

The oxpeckers benefit from a food source, while the impalas get relief from pests.

33.

Impalas are known to adapt their behavior based on their habitat and the presence of predators.

34.

They are capable swimmers and will enter water bodies to escape predators or find food.

35.

Impalas communicate with each other through vocalizations, body language, and scent-marking.

36.

They have a hierarchy within their herds, with dominant males leading and controlling access to resources.

37.

During the dry season, impalas are often seen near water sources, as they need to drink daily.

38.

The impala's diet consists of a variety of grasses and forbs, and they are selective feeders.

39.

The name "impala" is derived from the Zulu and Tswana languages, meaning "gazelle" or "antelope."

40.

The impala's adaptability and resilience have made them a common sight in many African national parks and reserves.

41.

They are a valuable resource for local communities, providing both sustenance and economic opportunities through ecotourism.

42.

Impalas' reproductive strategy of delayed implantation allows them to better allocate resources for raising their young.

43.

Their reddish-brown coloration changes seasonally to help them blend into their environment.

44.

Impalas have a relatively short lifespan in the wild, usually around 10 to 12 years.

45.

Their scientific name, Aepyceros melampus, translates to "high-horned" and "black-footed," respectively.

46.

They are considered an "edge species," often found on the boundaries between different habitats.

47.

In some cultures, impalas are considered symbols of grace, speed, and adaptability.

48.

They have a unique circulatory system that helps regulate their body temperature in extreme conditions.

49.

Impalas have been observed engaging in grooming behaviors, helping to maintain social bonds within herds.

50.

Their ability to thrive in a variety of environments makes impalas an iconic species of the African savanna.

51.

The Indian Cuckoo (Cuculus micropterus) is a medium-sized bird belonging to the cuckoo family, Cuculidae.

52.

This bird species is known for its distinctive and repetitive "cuckoo" call, which gives it its common name.

53.

The Indian Cuckoo is a brood parasite, meaning it lays its eggs in the nests of other bird species, leaving the host birds to raise its chicks.

54.

They are migratory birds, spending their breeding season in the Indian subcontinent and migrating to Africa during the non-breeding season.

55.

Indian Cuckoos have a slender body with a pointed tail, making them agile in flight.

56.

The male Indian Cuckoo has a glossy blue-black plumage, while the female has a brownish-grey coloration.

57.

Their diet primarily consists of insects, especially caterpillars, which they catch in mid-air or pluck from foliage.

58.

Indian Cuckoos are known to mimic the calls of other bird species, including the calls of birds of prey, to deter predators from approaching their nests.

59.

They have a unique ability to alter their vocalizations, imitating different bird species' calls, which helps them deceive host birds into thinking they are part of their own species.

60.

The breeding season for Indian Cuckoos is during the monsoon months when insect availability is high.

61.

The female Indian Cuckoo lays her eggs in the nests of other bird species, such as babblers, warblers, and prinias.

62.

Once the host bird raises the cuckoo chick, it often out-competes the host's own chicks due to its aggressive behavior and rapid growth.

63.

The Indian Cuckoo's eggs closely resemble the eggs of the host bird, reducing the chances of the host detecting the parasitic egg.

64.

The parasitic behavior of Indian Cuckoos can negatively impact the host bird population, especially if the cuckoo chicks outnumber the host's own chicks.

65.

Despite being brood parasites, Indian Cuckoos play a role in controlling insect populations, particularly during the breeding season.

66.

They are commonly found in forests, woodlands, scrublands, and open grassy habitats.

67.

Indian Cuckoos have a strong and rapid flight, and they are known to fly long distances during migration.

68.

The scientific name "Cuculus micropterus" is derived from Latin, where "Cuculus" refers to cuckoos and "micropterus" means "small-winged."

69.

They are known by various regional names, such as the "Papiha" in Hindi and "Kokila" in Bengali.

70.

The Indian Cuckoo's call is often associated with the arrival of the monsoon season, and its call is a familiar sound in rural and forested areas.

71.

The Indian Cuckoo's song is often used as a metaphor in Indian poetry and literature, symbolizing the arrival of rain and the changing seasons.

72.

They are sometimes mistaken for other bird species due to their ability to mimic different calls.

73.

The Indian Cuckoo is an intriguing example of evolutionary adaptations in avian behavior and reproductive strategies.

74.

They have been the subject of scientific studies exploring their mimicry and parasitic behavior.

75.

Indian Cuckoos face challenges due to habitat loss and the impact of climate change on their migratory patterns.

76.

Conservation efforts are focused on preserving their breeding and wintering habitats to ensure their survival.

77.

Indian Cuckoos play a role in pollination by feeding on nectar-rich flowers during their migration.

78.

Their presence can indicate the health of the ecosystem they inhabit, as they are sensitive to changes in habitat and food availability.

79.

The Indian Cuckoo's parasitic behavior has fascinated scientists and researchers for centuries.

80.

They are part of the intricate web of species interactions in ecosystems, influencing both host birds and insect populations.

81.

Indian Cuckoos exhibit a range of vocalizations beyond their iconic "cuckoo" call, including whistles, chatters, and trills.

82.

Their vocal mimicry is an example of convergent evolution, where different species develop similar traits due to similar ecological niches.

83.

The Indian Cuckoo is an example of how evolution has led to a diverse array of reproductive strategies in birds.

84.

Their migration between different continents highlights the interconnectedness of ecosystems across the globe.

85.

Indian Cuckoos are sometimes featured in local folklore, myths, and stories due to their unique behavior and vocalizations.

86.

These birds have been depicted in traditional art and cultural expressions in various regions.

87.

The Indian Cuckoo's ability to mimic other birds' calls has inspired artists and poets to create artistic representations and literary works.

88.

Their behavior raises ethical questions about the impact of parasitism on host bird populations and broader ecosystem dynamics.

89.

The Indian Cuckoo's parasitic behavior challenges our understanding of reproductive strategies and coevolution in bird species.

90.

Their behavior has been a subject of interest not only in the field of ornithology but also in the study of ecology and evolution.

91.

The Indian Cuckoo's interactions with other bird species reveal the complex ecological relationships that exist within ecosystems.

92.

They provide valuable insights into the evolution of mimicry and deception strategies in the natural world.

93.

Indian Cuckoos are not only fascinating from a biological perspective but also offer cultural and aesthetic value.

94.

The conservation of Indian Cuckoos highlights the importance of preserving biodiversity and maintaining healthy ecosystems.

95.

Efforts to protect Indian Cuckoos contribute to the overall health and stability of the ecosystems they inhabit.

96.

They are part of a larger network of species that contribute to the functioning of ecosystems and the services they provide.

97.

The Indian Cuckoo's behavior challenges our understanding of what it means to be a "parent" and how reproduction is achieved in the animal kingdom.

98.

Their parasitic behavior has implications for the study of parental care, altruism, and conflict in the avian world.

99.

Studying the Indian Cuckoo sheds light on the intricate interactions between different species and the factors that drive their evolution.

100.

The Indian Cuckoo serves as a reminder of the complexity and beauty of the natural world, encouraging us to continue exploring and learning about the organisms that share our planet.

101.

NASDAQ, short for the National Association of Securities Dealers Automated Quotations, was founded on February 8, 1971.

102.

It was the world's first electronic stock market and introduced automated trading systems.

103.

NASDAQ initially began as a quotation system to provide real-time stock prices to brokers and dealers.

104.

The first stock traded on NASDAQ was "Spectra Physics," a laser manufacturer.

105.

The NASDAQ Composite Index was introduced in 1971 as well, representing all the companies listed on the NASDAQ stock exchange.

106.

NASDAQ is known for its electronic trading platform, allowing for fast and efficient transactions.

107.

In 2000, NASDAQ merged with the American Stock Exchange (AMEX), but the merger was short-lived due to regulatory challenges.

108.

The NASDAQ stock exchange is headquartered in New York City, with additional offices around the world.

109.

NASDAQ has been a leader in technology and innovation, pioneering electronic trading methods and data dissemination.

110.

It played a significant role in democratizing stock trading by making information more accessible to retail investors.

111.

In the 1990s, NASDAQ was associated with the dot-com bubble, as many technology-related companies were listed on the exchange.

112.

The NASDAQ-100 Index was introduced in 1985, comprising the 100 largest non-financial companies listed on NASDAQ.

113.

NASDAQ is known for its all-electronic trading system, contrasting with traditional stock exchanges that had physical trading floors.

114.

The exchange uses market makers to facilitate trades by matching buy and sell orders.

115.

NASDAQ's trading hours are from 9:30 AM to 4:00 PM Eastern
Time.

116.

NASDAQ introduced the Small Order Execution System (SOES) in
1984, which allowed investors to trade smaller orders electronically.

117.

In 1999, NASDAQ acquired the London International Financial
Futures and Options Exchange (LIFFE) to expand its global reach.

118.

The NASDAQ Stock Market was officially recognized as a stock
exchange by the U.S. Securities and Exchange Commission (SEC) in
2006.

119.

NASDAQ played a key role in shaping electronic trading platforms,
influencing other stock exchanges to adopt similar systems.

120.

It is known for its competitive listing fees, attracting tech-focused
companies and startups.

121.

NASDAQ introduced the Nasdaq-100 European Tracker Fund,
allowing European investors to trade in the NASDAQ-100 Index.

122.

The exchange was involved in several high-profile tech IPOs,
including Apple, Microsoft, Amazon, and Google (now Alphabet).

123.

NASDAQ is also known for its vibrant trading floors in various locations, featuring digital displays of stock information.

124.

In 2016, NASDAQ acquired the International Securities Exchange (ISE), enhancing its options trading capabilities.

125.

NASDAQ has expanded beyond equities trading to include options, futures, and other financial products.

126.

The NASDAQ MarketSite in Times Square, New York City, is a famous landmark known for displaying stock market data and corporate events.

127.

In 2020, NASDAQ introduced the "Purpose Initiative" to drive positive change in environmental, social, and governance (ESG) areas.

128.

NASDAQ's SMARTS technology is used for market surveillance and monitoring for potential market abuses.

129.

The exchange hosts various indices, including the NASDAQ-100, NASDAQ Composite, and NASDAQ Biotechnology Index.

130.

NASDAQ introduced the MarketSite Tower in Times Square, providing a massive digital display for stock market information.

131.

In 2019, NASDAQ acquired eVestment, a provider of institutional investment data and analytics.

132.

The "opening bell" ceremony at NASDAQ is a renowned tradition, featuring company executives and celebrities ringing the bell to mark the start of trading.

133.

NASDAQ has continuously evolved its trading systems to ensure high speed, efficiency, and reliability.

134.

It has a significant role in shaping market structure and modernizing the financial industry.

135.

In 2008, NASDAQ OMX Group was formed after the merger of NASDAQ and the OMX stock exchange group.

136.

NASDAQ OMX Group is also involved in providing technology solutions to other stock exchanges globally.

137.

NASDAQ's branding is synonymous with technology, innovation, and the growth of the tech industry.

138.

The exchange has hosted many "unicorns" (privately held startups valued at over $1 billion) as they went public.

139.

NASDAQ operates under the oversight of the U.S. SEC to ensure fair and transparent trading practices.

140.

The NASDAQ-100 Index includes companies from various sectors, including technology, consumer services, healthcare, and more.

141.

The exchange faced challenges during the 2010 "Flash Crash," which led to a temporary halt in trading.

142.

NASDAQ was involved in pioneering decimalization in the early 2000s, transitioning from fractions to decimal pricing for stock quotes.

143.

NASDAQ has been a hub for innovation, often attracting companies that are at the forefront of technological advancements.

144.

In 2007, NASDAQ launched the NASDAQ OMX Green Economy Index, reflecting the growing interest in sustainability.

145.

NASDAQ has also been involved in philanthropy and community initiatives, supporting educational programs and charitable efforts.

146.

The NASDAQ stock exchange has become a symbol of modern finance, representing the shift from traditional trading floors to electronic systems.

147.

The exchange has been at the forefront of adapting to technological advancements, including algorithmic trading and high-frequency trading.

148.

NASDAQ's electronic trading platform has contributed to the increased liquidity and accessibility of financial markets.

149.

The NASDAQ market has witnessed numerous market milestones, reflecting the ups and downs of the global economy.

150.

NASDAQ's history is a testament to the power of innovation, technology, and adaptation in the financial industry, shaping the way we trade and invest today.

151.

The Dole Food Company, Inc., commonly known as Dole, was founded in 1851 by James Drummond Dole.

152.

Dole is a global food and beverage company specializing in fruits, vegetables, and packaged foods.

153.

The company's first operations were focused on selling pineapples and other tropical fruits in Hawaii.

154.

Dole played a significant role in popularizing and commercializing the pineapple industry in Hawaii.

155.

Dole's iconic logo featuring a pineapple became synonymous with quality fruit products.

156.

In the early 20th century, Dole expanded its operations to include the cultivation and canning of pineapples for worldwide distribution.

157.

The "Dole Hawaiian Pineapple Company" was established in 1901.

158.

Dole introduced innovations in packaging and transportation that allowed fresh pineapples to reach markets around the world.

159.

In the 1920s, Dole pioneered the concept of the "Pineapple Train," a tour train that showcased its pineapple plantations to visitors.

160.

Dole's pineapple plantations became a symbol of Hawaii's agricultural industry and contributed to the state's economy.

161.

Dole's role in the pineapple industry led to the title "Pineapple King" for its founder, James Dole.

162.

Dole's expansion beyond pineapples began in the 1920s when it started growing and selling bananas as well.

163.

In 1961, Dole introduced the first canned pineapple juice to the market.

164.

Dole continued to diversify its product offerings to include other fruits, vegetables, and packaged foods.

165.

The company expanded its operations to other countries, including the Philippines, Costa Rica, and Ecuador.

166.

Dole was acquired by Castle & Cooke in 1961, leading to its global expansion.

167.

Dole became a publicly-traded company in 2009 when it filed for an initial public offering (IPO).

168.

The company's IPO marked its return to the public markets after being privately held for several years.

169.

Dole has faced controversies over its labor practices and environmental impact in certain regions.

170.

The company has made efforts to address sustainability concerns, such as implementing responsible farming practices and reducing waste.

171.

Dole is one of the world's largest producers and marketers of fresh fruit and vegetables.

172.

The company's products include fresh and packaged fruits, vegetables, salads, juices, and more.

173.

Dole has been recognized for its commitment to food safety and quality assurance standards.

174.

The "Dole 5 A Day" campaign, launched in the 1990s, aimed to encourage healthy eating habits by promoting the consumption of fruits and vegetables.

175.

Dole's involvement in the banana industry led to its recognition as one of the "Big Four" banana companies.

176.

Dole's banana plantations have been the subject of debate regarding labor conditions and workers' rights.

177.

In 2013, Dole announced plans to sell its packaged foods and Asian fresh fruit businesses to focus on fresh produce.

178.

Dole has been involved in various corporate social responsibility initiatives, including supporting local communities and disaster relief efforts.

179.

The company has faced financial challenges, including debt and declining profits, in various periods of its history.

180.

Dole's presence in the European market was bolstered through its acquisition of the European fruit company, Standard Fruit.

181.

Dole has been recognized for its efforts in reducing the environmental impact of its operations, including water conservation and waste reduction.

182.

The company's "Dole Promise" outlines its commitment to sustainability, transparency, and improved nutrition.

183.

Dole has expanded its product lines to include organic and non-GMO options in response to consumer demand.

184.

Dole's banana plantations have been impacted by diseases, such as the Panama disease, leading to efforts to develop disease-resistant banana varieties.

185.

Dole has also been involved in philanthropic efforts, including providing funding for education and healthcare programs in various countries.

186.

In 2018, Dole announced a partnership with the World Wildlife Fund (WWF) to improve the sustainability of its supply chain.

187.

The company's headquarters have been located in various places over its history, including Hawaii, California, and North Carolina.

188.

Dole's products are sold in grocery stores, supermarkets, and foodservice establishments worldwide.

189.

The company has explored innovative packaging solutions to extend the shelf life of its products and reduce food waste.

190.

Dole's involvement in the fruit industry has contributed to the development of global trade networks and supply chains.

191.

Dole's pineapple plantations in Hawaii have become tourist attractions, allowing visitors to see the cultivation process and learn about the history of the industry.

192.

The company's focus on sustainability has led to initiatives aimed at reducing carbon emissions, conserving water, and protecting biodiversity.

193.

Dole's history is intertwined with the history of Hawaii, where it played a vital role in shaping the agricultural landscape.

194.

The company's commitment to providing nutritious and accessible food aligns with changing consumer preferences toward healthier eating habits.

195.

Dole's acquisition by Total Produce in 2018 resulted in the formation of the world's largest fresh produce company.

196.

The Dole Nutrition Institute was established to provide information and resources about the health benefits of fruits and vegetables.

197.

Dole has launched various advertising and marketing campaigns to promote its products, often highlighting the natural goodness of its fruits.

198.

The company's reach extends to both retail and foodservice sectors, supplying a wide range of customers.

199.

Dole has weathered challenges in the industry, such as changing consumer trends and competitive pressures.

200.

The company's legacy as a pioneer in the fruit industry continues to influence the way fruits and vegetables are grown, processed, and distributed worldwide.

201.

The Yale Bowl is a historic football stadium located in New Haven, Connecticut, on the campus of Yale University.

202.

It is one of the oldest active football stadiums in the United States, with a rich history dating back to its opening in 1914.

203.

The Yale Bowl was designed by architect Charles A. Ferry, who aimed to create a state-of-the-art football stadium at the time.

204.

It was constructed using the "bowl" design concept, which involves excavating the ground to create a natural amphitheater-like setting for spectators.

205.

The Yale Bowl was the first college football stadium in the country to use this innovative design.

206.

The stadium has a seating capacity of around 61,446, making it one of the largest college football stadiums in the Northeast.

207.

The original cost of building the Yale Bowl was approximately $750,000.

208.

The stadium's official name is the "Yale Bowl," but it is also commonly referred to as the "The Bowl."

209.

The Yale Bowl has hosted numerous football games, including Yale University's home football games and other college football events.

210.

It was designated as a National Historic Landmark in 1987 due to its architectural significance and historical importance.

211.

The first game ever played at the Yale Bowl was between Yale and Harvard on November 21, 1914.

212.

The Yale Bowl's inaugural game drew a crowd of over 70,000 spectators, a testament to its popularity and importance in college football.

213.

The stadium's playing surface is made of natural grass.

214.

The Yale Bowl has also hosted soccer matches, concerts, and other events over the years.

215.

It was the site of the National Football League's (NFL) All-Star Game in 1938.

216.

The Yale Bowl's seating structure was designed to provide clear sightlines and unobstructed views for all spectators.

217.

The stadium's open-air design gives fans a unique experience of watching games in a historic setting.

218.

The Yale Bowl was one of the first football stadiums to feature a press box, which provided space for journalists and broadcasters to cover the games.

219.

The stadium's architecture is characterized by its distinctive horseshoe shape and Neo-Gothic details.

220.

The Yale Bowl has been referenced in literature, movies, and television shows as an iconic football venue.

221.

It has a rich rivalry with the Harvard Stadium, often referred to as "The Game," which is the annual football game between Yale and Harvard.

222.

The Yale Bowl has seen renovations and updates over the years to enhance its facilities and maintain its historical integrity.

223.

The stadium has been used as a backdrop for various historical events and celebrations.

224.

The Yale Bowl's classic design has influenced the construction of other football stadiums across the country.

225.

The stadium's location on the Yale University campus makes it an integral part of the university's history and traditions.

226.

The Yale Bowl was used as a training facility for the U.S. military during World War I and World War II.

227.

The stadium's archways and Gothic details give it a timeless and elegant appearance.

228.

The Yale Bowl's historical significance extends beyond football, as it represents an architectural and cultural milestone.

229.

It has been the site of various halftime shows, marching band performances, and other entertainment events.

230.

The Yale Bowl's proximity to the Yale Art Gallery and other cultural attractions adds to its appeal as a destination for visitors.

231.

The stadium's seating capacity has been adjusted over the years to accommodate changing safety regulations and comfort standards.

232.

The Yale Bowl's capacity has been temporarily expanded for certain high-profile games and events.

233.

The stadium's bowl-shaped design allows for excellent crowd acoustics, enhancing the atmosphere during games.

234.

The Yale Bowl's rich history and iconic architecture have contributed to its recognition as a National Historic Landmark.

235.

The venue's tradition of hosting football games during the fall season continues to attract fans from Yale and opposing teams.

236.

The Yale Bowl has been the stage for memorable moments in college football history, including notable plays and victories.

237.

The stadium's historic significance has led to efforts to preserve its original features while modernizing its facilities.

238.

The Yale Bowl's exterior features intricate stone carvings and ornamental details that reflect the craftsmanship of the time.

239.

The stadium has been featured in documentaries and media coverage highlighting its role in the evolution of football stadiums.

240.

The Yale Bowl's unique design has contributed to its recognition as a landmark of American sports architecture.

241.

The stadium's horseshoe layout encourages a sense of camaraderie among fans and players alike.

242.

The Yale Bowl's classic appearance contrasts with modern stadiums, offering a glimpse into the past.

243.

The stadium's design allows for efficient crowd movement and easy access to seating areas.

244.

The Yale Bowl's proximity to downtown New Haven makes it accessible to visitors exploring the city's cultural attractions.

245.

The stadium's historical plaques and markers provide insights into its construction and significance.

246.

The Yale Bowl's architectural features pay homage to the university's traditions and academic excellence.

247.

The stadium's presence on the Yale campus has made it a cherished gathering place for alumni, students, and fans.

248.

The Yale Bowl's legacy extends to its role as a symbol of Yale's commitment to athletics and education.

249.

The stadium's setting within a picturesque campus landscape adds to its visual appeal.

250.

The Yale Bowl remains a living testament to the enduring legacy of college football and the cultural significance of sports architecture.

251.

The first telephone exchange was established in New Haven, Connecticut, USA, on January 28, 1878.

252.

It was founded by George W. Coy, who was the head of the District Telephone Company of New Haven.

253.

The exchange had just 21 subscribers initially, all within a three-mile radius.

254.

The first telephone exchange operated from the offices of the District Telephone Company.

255.

The exchange used manual switching, where operators physically connected calls by plugging and unplugging cables.

256.

The first telephone exchange was a response to the growing number of telephones in the area, making direct communication between subscribers difficult.

257.

The idea of a telephone exchange was promoted by George W. Coy and his friend Elisha Gray.

258.

The first exchange's operators were young women who were skilled in operating the switchboards.

259.

The first exchange was open for business for only a few hours each day initially.

260.

The first telephone exchange was a major breakthrough that enabled subscribers to connect with each other more efficiently.

261.

In 1879, there were 12 more telephone exchanges established in various cities across the United States.

262.

The first exchange marked the beginning of the concept of centralized communication hubs that facilitated multiple connections.

263.

The first telephone exchange utilized a manual system where operators used plugs and cords to connect calls.

264.

The first exchange faced challenges such as limited coverage area and the need for skilled operators.

265.

The concept of a telephone exchange revolutionized communication by allowing multiple parties to communicate simultaneously.

266.

The success of the first telephone exchange laid the foundation for the rapid expansion of telephone networks worldwide.

267.

Within a few years, other countries adopted the telephone exchange system, enhancing global communication.

268.

The first telephone exchange paved the way for the eventual automation and digitization of switching systems.

269.

The introduction of the telephone exchange system sparked the growth of telecommunication companies and industries.

270.

The first telephone exchange brought about a paradigm shift in how people communicated, fostering social and economic changes.

271.

The expansion of telephone exchanges facilitated long-distance communication, transforming business and personal interactions.

272.

The first exchange was a vital step towards making telecommunication services accessible to the general public.

273.

As telephone exchanges multiplied, the need for standardized equipment and protocols emerged.

274.

The concept of a telephone exchange was instrumental in promoting the idea of a universal numbering system for telephones.

275.

The first exchange demonstrated the potential of telecommunication technology and paved the way for future innovations.

276.

The telephone exchange system played a crucial role in breaking down geographical barriers and connecting communities.

277.

The success of the first exchange inspired inventors and engineers to improve and refine telephone technology.

278.

The first telephone exchange laid the groundwork for the establishment of a telecommunication infrastructure that is now ubiquitous.

279.

The manual operation of the first exchange required operators to have a deep understanding of the local community.

280.

The first exchange was a precursor to the development of more advanced telecommunication networks, including digital switching.

281.

The establishment of telephone exchanges marked the transition from isolated point-to-point communication to a networked system.

282.

The first exchange introduced the idea of a central hub where calls were managed, directing them to their intended recipients.

283.

The manual labor involved in the first exchange's operations highlighted the need for automation and innovation.

284.

The introduction of telephone exchanges spurred a wave of patents and technological advancements in the telecommunication field.

285.

The first exchange enabled businesses to conduct transactions more efficiently and communicate with suppliers and customers.

286.

The first exchange's impact on society was profound, accelerating the pace of information sharing and decision-making.

287.

The success of the first telephone exchange inspired entrepreneurs to invest in telecommunication infrastructure.

288.

The introduction of telephone exchanges fueled competition among telecommunication companies, leading to improved services.

289.

The first exchange's reliance on human operators underscored the importance of developing automated switching systems.

290.

The establishment of telephone exchanges marked a critical turning point in the history of telecommunications.

291.

The manual nature of the first exchange's operations required operators to have a keen memory and multitasking skills.

292.

The first exchange encouraged further research and development in telecommunication technology.

293.

The idea of a telephone exchange system spread rapidly, with countries around the world adopting similar concepts.

294.

The first exchange's success demonstrated the potential of telecommunication technology to drive economic growth.

295.

The concept of a telephone exchange paved the way for the integration of telephony into daily life and business operations.

296.

The first exchange highlighted the importance of standardizing procedures and protocols for efficient communication.

297.

The growth of telephone exchanges facilitated the creation of local and national telephone networks.

298.

The first exchange's limited capacity and reliance on operators led to ongoing efforts to improve efficiency and expand coverage.

299.

The establishment of telephone exchanges played a crucial role in shaping the modern telecommunication landscape.

300.

The legacy of the first telephone exchange is evident in the seamless global communication systems we enjoy today.

301.

The Indian Rhinoceros (Rhinoceros unicornis) is one of the largest land mammals, second only to the African Elephant.

302.

They are primarily found in the Indian subcontinent, including India, Nepal, and Bhutan.

303.

Indian Rhinoceroses have a single horn on their snouts, unlike African rhinos that can have two.

304.

The horn of an Indian Rhinoceros is made of keratin, similar to human hair and nails.

305.

They are herbivores and mainly feed on grasses, fruits, leaves, and aquatic plants.

306.

The Indian Rhinoceros has thick, grayish-brown skin that is heavily folded, giving it a unique appearance.

307.

Adult Indian Rhinoceroses can weigh between 2,000 to 3,000 kg (4,400 to 6,600 lbs).

308.

They have a distinctive hump on their shoulders, which distinguishes them from other rhino species.

309.

Despite their massive size, Indian Rhinoceroses are surprisingly agile and can run at speeds of up to 40 km/h (25 mph).

310.

They are excellent swimmers and can even dive underwater, using their prehensile upper lip as a snorkel.

311.

Indian Rhinoceroses have poor eyesight but a keen sense of hearing and a strong sense of smell.

312.

These rhinos are known for their territorial behavior and often mark their territories with dung piles and urine.

313.

Indian Rhinoceroses have a symbiotic relationship with certain birds, like the Indian Oxpecker, which feeds on parasites and insects from their skin.

314.

Their population was once severely threatened due to habitat loss and hunting, but conservation efforts have helped increase their numbers.

315.

Kaziranga National Park in Assam, India, is a renowned habitat for Indian Rhinoceroses and has played a significant role in their conservation.

316.

Indian Rhinoceroses have been listed as Vulnerable on the IUCN Red List due to habitat loss and poaching for their horns.

317.

Conservation efforts have helped increase their population to around 3,600 individuals as of the latest estimates.

318.

They have a solitary nature and are typically seen alone, except for mothers with their calves.

319.

Female Indian Rhinoceroses have a longer and more slender horn compared to males.

320.

Mating behavior can be aggressive, with males engaging in fights to establish dominance.

321.

The gestation period for Indian Rhinoceroses is around 16 months, and females give birth to a single calf.

322.

Calves are born with a reddish-brown coat that gradually changes to the characteristic gray as they grow.

323.

Indian Rhinoceroses have a lifespan of around 40 to 50 years in the wild.

324.

They are listed in Appendix I of the Convention on International Trade in Endangered Species (CITES), which means their trade is highly regulated.

325.

The Indian Rhinoceros has played a significant role in local cultures and folklore, often symbolizing power and strength.

326.

The Indian Rhino Vision 2020 is a conservation program aiming to increase the population of Indian Rhinoceroses in Assam to 3,000 by 2020.

327.

Despite their size, Indian Rhinoceroses are known to be good climbers and can navigate steep inclines.

328.

In 2018, the population of Indian Rhinoceroses in Kaziranga National Park reached a milestone of 2,413 individuals.

329.

Their thick folds of skin help them retain moisture and keep cool in the hot and humid climate of their habitat.

330.

Indian Rhinoceroses have a prehensile upper lip that they use to grasp and pull vegetation into their mouths.

331.

They are crepuscular, which means they are most active during the early morning and late afternoon.

332.

Unlike some other rhino species, Indian Rhinoceroses are not known for their aggressive behavior towards humans.

333.

Indian Rhinoceroses have been a subject of various conservation initiatives, including captive breeding programs.

334.

The success of the Indian Rhinoceros conservation efforts showcases the positive impact of collaborative efforts between governments, NGOs, and local communities.

335.

Their wallowing behavior helps them cool off, protect their skin from parasites, and mark their territories.

336.

Indian Rhinoceroses communicate with each other through a variety of vocalizations, including roars, grunts, and squeaks.

337.

They have a dense patch of hair on their ears, which helps keep insects away.

338.

Indian Rhinoceroses are essential in maintaining the health of their ecosystem by shaping the vegetation and creating habitat for other species.

339.

These rhinos have thick, strong legs with three toes on each foot, which makes them well-suited for walking in muddy terrain.

340.

The Indian Rhinoceros is a flagship species, attracting attention and resources to its habitat and benefiting other species in the process.

341.

Their conservation status improved from Endangered to Vulnerable due to successful conservation efforts.

342.

Indian Rhinoceroses face threats such as habitat loss, illegal wildlife trade, and human-wildlife conflict.

343.

Despite their large size, Indian Rhinoceroses are surprisingly agile and can maneuver through dense vegetation.

344.

The rhino's horn has cultural significance in traditional medicine and is erroneously believed to have curative properties.

345.

In 1987, the Manas Wildlife Sanctuary in Assam was declared a UNESCO Natural World Heritage site, further protecting the Indian Rhinoceros habitat.

346.

Indian Rhinoceroses have a relatively slow reproductive rate, with females typically giving birth every three to four years.

347.

Rhino conservation efforts are often intertwined with local livelihoods, focusing on providing alternative sources of income to reduce human-wildlife conflict.

348.

The Indian Rhinoceros has been depicted in various art forms, literature, and films, contributing to its cultural significance.

349.

India's Project Rhino was launched in 1992 with the goal of conserving and managing Indian Rhinoceros populations and their habitats.

350.

Conservation organizations and governments continue to work together to secure the future of Indian Rhinoceroses by addressing the ongoing challenges they face.

351.

The Indian Skimmer is a distinctive bird known for its remarkable feeding behavior, where it skims the water surface with its lower mandible to catch fish.

352.

This bird is also known as the "Scissor-Billed Tern" due to its unique bill shape and feeding technique.

353.

Indian Skimmers are medium-sized birds with a length of about 40-45 cm and a wingspan of approximately 100 cm.

354.

They have a black cap, a white body, and a distinctive black collar on the nape.

355.

The lower mandible of the Indian Skimmer's bill is longer than the upper mandible, enabling it to glide just above the water's surface.

356.

The skimming action of the Indian Skimmer's bill creates a wake that helps it detect and catch fish.

357.

They have long, pointed wings and a forked tail, which aids in their swift and agile flight.

358.

Indian Skimmers are found in riverine habitats, especially along large rivers, lakes, and reservoirs.

359.

They are highly social birds and often nest in colonies, creating a sense of community.

360.

Indian Skimmers are primarily found in South Asian countries, including India, Bangladesh, Nepal, and parts of Southeast Asia.

361.

Their preferred habitats are sandbanks and gravel bars along riverbanks where they nest and roost.

362.

During the breeding season, Indian Skimmers form pairs, and both parents contribute to incubating the eggs and caring for the young.

363.

Their nests are simple scrapes in the sand, sometimes lined with small pebbles or shells.

364.

Indian Skimmers lay two to four eggs in a clutch.

365.

The chicks are born with cryptic down feathers that help them blend into their sandy surroundings.

366.

Their diet consists almost entirely of fish, which they catch by skimming the water's surface.

367.

They are known to feed cooperatively, flying in groups over the water and herding fish into shallower areas for easier capture.

368.

Indian Skimmers are often seen resting on sandbanks or logs during the day, especially during the heat of midday.

369.

The species is listed as "Vulnerable" on the IUCN Red List due to habitat loss and disturbances at their breeding sites.

370.

They are susceptible to disturbances from humans, including boating, fishing, and recreational activities.

371.

Conservation efforts are focused on protecting their nesting sites, raising awareness about their unique behavior, and promoting responsible ecotourism.

372.

Indian Skimmers are mainly active during the early morning and late afternoon, avoiding the hottest parts of the day.

373.

Their distinctive black collar and white body make Indian Skimmers easily distinguishable from other bird species.

374.

They have a distinctive call, a series of repetitive barking-like sounds.

375.

The Indian Skimmer has a strong visual presence with its striking coloration and unique bill shape.

376.

During the non-breeding season, Indian Skimmers may gather in larger flocks, sometimes comprising hundreds of individuals.

377.

They face threats such as habitat degradation, sand mining, and disturbance by humans and domestic animals.

378.

The Indian Skimmer's population is estimated to be declining due to ongoing threats to their habitat.

379.

Conservationists work with local communities to promote sustainable fishing practices and minimize disturbances to nesting sites.

380.

Their distribution is largely tied to river systems, and their health reflects the overall health of these ecosystems.

381.

Indian Skimmers have been studied to better understand their behavior, migration patterns, and breeding ecology.

382.

They often roost on sandbanks and islands in rivers, where they can rest safely away from potential predators.

383.

Indian Skimmers have a graceful flight pattern, gliding low over the water's surface as they search for fish.

384.

The species was previously considered part of the "Rynchops" genus but was later reclassified under the "Eurylaimidae" family.

385.

They are known to migrate short distances within their range in response to changes in water levels.

386.

Their specialized bill adaptation is a marvel of evolution, allowing them to thrive in specific habitats.

387.

Indian Skimmers are elusive birds and can be difficult to spot due to their habit of resting and nesting on sandbanks away from human activity.

388.

The loss of suitable nesting sites due to riverbank erosion is a significant threat to their survival.

389.

Successful conservation initiatives include establishing protected areas along rivers and educating local communities about the importance of their habitat.

390.

Indian Skimmers play a role in maintaining the ecological balance of aquatic ecosystems by controlling fish populations.

391.

As ecosystem indicators, the presence and abundance of Indian Skimmers reflect the overall health of river ecosystems.

392.

Their captivating behavior and unique appearance make Indian Skimmers popular subjects for birdwatching and ecotourism.

393.

Conservation organizations collaborate to monitor their populations and raise awareness about their conservation needs.

394.

The Indian Skimmer's scientific name, "Rynchops albicollis," is derived from Greek and Latin words that describe its bill and white collar.

395.

Their presence has cultural significance for local communities, highlighting the importance of preserving natural habitats.

396.

The Indian Skimmer's habitat range overlaps with other water-associated bird species, contributing to the overall biodiversity of these areas.

397.

These birds have a strong fidelity to their nesting sites, often returning to the same location year after year.

398.

They are affected by changes in water flow, pollution, and alterations to river systems caused by human activities.

399.

Conservation efforts also address the needs of local communities to strike a balance between sustainable development and protecting these birds.

400.

The Indian Skimmer serves as a reminder of the interconnectedness of species and ecosystems, motivating efforts to preserve their unique behaviors and habitats.

401.

SpaceX was founded with the ambitious goal of reducing space transportation costs and enabling the colonization of Mars.

402.

Elon Musk, known for his roles in companies like PayPal and Tesla, co-founded SpaceX and has been its driving force since its inception.

403.

The company's headquarters is located in Hawthorne, California, near Los Angeles.

404.

SpaceX's first launch vehicle was the Falcon 1, which became the first privately developed liquid-fueled rocket to reach Earth orbit in 2008.

405.

In 2010, SpaceX successfully launched its Falcon 9 rocket, which was designed for reusability and cost efficiency.

406.

Falcon 9's first stage is designed to land vertically back on Earth after launch, a breakthrough innovation in rocket technology.

407.

The Dragon spacecraft, developed by SpaceX, became the first commercial spacecraft to deliver cargo to the International Space Station (ISS) in 2012.

408.

In 2015, SpaceX achieved the first successful landing of a Falcon 9 first stage back on land.

409.

Reusability of rocket components has become a cornerstone of SpaceX's cost-saving strategy.

410.

Falcon Heavy, introduced in 2018, is one of the most powerful rockets ever built, capable of carrying large payloads to various orbits.

411.

SpaceX's Starship is an upcoming fully reusable spacecraft designed for missions to Mars and beyond. It's intended to replace the Falcon 9 and Falcon Heavy.

412.

In 2020, SpaceX successfully launched two American astronauts, Bob Behnken and Doug Hurley, to the ISS aboard the Crew Dragon spacecraft.

413.

This Crew Dragon mission marked the first crewed launch from American soil since the Space Shuttle program ended in 2011.

414.

The Starlink project aims to create a global satellite network to provide high-speed internet access to remote and underserved areas.

415.

SpaceX launches batches of Starlink satellites on Falcon 9 rockets, gradually increasing the size of the constellation.

416.

SpaceX has significantly lowered the cost of launching payloads into space, making it more accessible for other companies and organizations.

417.

The company has a track record of winning contracts from NASA, the US Department of Defense, and commercial satellite operators.

418.

In 2017, SpaceX announced plans to send two private individuals on a mission around the Moon using the Crew Dragon spacecraft and Falcon Heavy.

419.

The company regularly conducts test flights of its vehicles and systems, embracing a "fail-fast" philosophy to improve and iterate quickly.

420.

SpaceX is known for its innovative culture and willingness to take on audacious challenges.

421.

Elon Musk's long-term vision for SpaceX is to establish a self-sustaining colony on Mars to ensure the survival of humanity in case of Earth's catastrophe.

422.

The development and operations of SpaceX have led to advancements in rocket propulsion, materials science, and manufacturing processes.

423.

The company's achievements have ignited competition and innovation within the aerospace industry.

424.

SpaceX's work has contributed to a renewed interest in space exploration and inspired a new generation of engineers, scientists, and space enthusiasts.

425.

The company has made historic progress toward commercializing space travel and reducing the cost barrier for launching payloads.

426.

SpaceX's Starship is designed to carry both crew and cargo, with the ultimate goal of making interplanetary travel a reality.

427.

The company's launch facilities include Cape Canaveral Space Force Station in Florida, Vandenberg Space Force Base in California, and a private launch site in Texas.

428.

SpaceX has worked on developing reusable technologies to reduce the environmental impact of space launches.

429.

The company has revolutionized the space industry by proving that reusing rocket components is economically viable.

430.

In 2021, SpaceX launched its first all-civilian mission, known as Inspiration4, sending four private individuals on a multi-day orbital journey.

431.

The Starship prototype, known as SN10, successfully completed a high-altitude test flight and landing in March 2021, marking a significant step toward Mars colonization.

432.

SpaceX's achievements have helped stimulate commercial space tourism initiatives, promoting the idea of private citizens traveling to space.

433.

The company actively collaborates with other space agencies and international partners to advance space exploration and technology.

434.

Elon Musk envisions a future where a city on Mars could become self-sustaining and serve as a backup for humanity's survival.

435.

SpaceX's rapid iteration and development approach have led to frequent updates and changes to its vehicles and systems.

436.

The company's innovation extends to its manufacturing processes, including the production of carbon fiber structures and advanced rocket engines.

437.

SpaceX's successes have also contributed to the reinvigoration of interest in lunar exploration, with the company being selected to deliver payloads to the Moon's surface as part of NASA's Artemis program.

438.

The company's launch cadence has increased significantly over the years, with multiple launches conducted each month.

439.

SpaceX's advancements in reusability have led to cost savings estimated to be over 70% compared to traditional expendable launch vehicles.

440.

The company's ambitious goals and progress have sparked the imaginations of people worldwide, leading to renewed interest in the space sector.

441.

SpaceX continues to innovate in its quest to make space travel and exploration more accessible and affordable.

442.

The company's work has fostered a competitive environment in the aerospace industry, driving other companies to explore new ways to reduce costs and improve technology.

443.

SpaceX's successful launches and missions have demonstrated the potential for the private sector to play a pivotal role in space exploration and development.

444.

The development of the Starship system has presented technical challenges, but SpaceX's iterative approach has allowed them to make significant strides.

445.

The company's dedication to landing and reusing rocket stages has become a hallmark of its launches, showcasing its commitment to sustainability and cost-efficiency.

446.

SpaceX's achievements have led to increased interest from governments, organizations, and private individuals in collaborating on space missions and projects.

447.

Elon Musk's vision of a multi-planetary species has inspired discussions about humanity's long-term future beyond Earth.

448.

The company's Mars colonization plans involve using the Starship system to transport large numbers of people and cargo to the Red Planet.

449.

SpaceX's work has had a transformative effect on the space launch market, leading to a new era of more frequent and cost-effective launches.

450.

As of 2023, SpaceX continues to develop and iterate on its vehicles, with an eye toward achieving Elon Musk's vision of enabling human settlement on Mars.

451.

RingCentral was founded in 1999 by Vlad Shmunis in San Mateo, California.

452.

The company initially focused on developing a cloud-based phone system for small businesses.

453.

RingCentral's first product was a virtual PBX system, allowing businesses to manage phone calls and communications without traditional hardware.

454.

The company's goal was to disrupt the traditional telecommunications industry by offering a more flexible and cost-effective alternative.

455.

In 2003, RingCentral launched its flagship product, RingCentral Office, which combined phone, video conferencing, and team messaging.

456.

Over the years, RingCentral expanded its offerings to include additional features like SMS, online faxing, and integrations with other business tools.

457.

The company went public in 2013, trading on the New York Stock Exchange under the ticker symbol "RNG."

458.

In 2015, RingCentral introduced the "Glip" team messaging and collaboration platform, which later became an integral part of its services.

459.

The company's cloud-based approach allowed businesses to scale their communication needs more easily without investing in hardware infrastructure.

460.

In 2017, RingCentral partnered with Google to integrate its services with Google Cloud, enhancing collaboration and communication for Google Workspace users.

461.

RingCentral's platform is designed to be accessible from various devices, including desktop computers, smartphones, and tablets.

462.

The company's technology allows for unified communication across voice, video conferencing, and messaging channels.

463.

In 2018, RingCentral partnered with Atos to offer a cloud-based communication solution for large enterprises.

464.

RingCentral's API platform enables developers to build custom integrations and applications using its communication services.

465.

The company's global expansion includes offices in various countries, supporting businesses with international communication needs.

466.

RingCentral's acquisition of Dimelo in 2018 enhanced its capabilities in digital customer engagement and social media interactions.

467.

The company's focus on innovation led to the development of AI-powered features, enhancing call routing and customer interactions.

468.

By integrating with leading CRM and business software solutions, RingCentral offers a seamless experience for users.

469.

In 2020, RingCentral acquired Avaya's cloud business, solidifying its position as a leader in the Unified Communications as a Service (UCaaS) market.

470.

RingCentral's partnership with Alcatel-Lucent Enterprise in 2021 expanded its communication offerings to more customers globally.

471.

The company's user-friendly interface and intuitive design make it accessible to businesses of all sizes and industries.

472.

RingCentral's services are tailored for various sectors, including healthcare, education, finance, and more.

473.

The platform's analytics and reporting features provide insights into call patterns, user behavior, and communication trends.

474.

The COVID-19 pandemic highlighted the importance of remote communication tools, driving increased adoption of RingCentral's services.

475.

The company's commitment to security includes encryption, compliance with industry regulations, and multi-factor authentication.

476.

RingCentral's "RingCentral Video" service offers secure video conferencing with features like screen sharing and recording.

477.

The company's "RingCentral Rooms" technology facilitates seamless video conferencing within physical meeting rooms.

478.

RingCentral's mobile app enables users to stay connected and communicate on the go.

479.

The company's customer support offers 24/7 assistance, reflecting its dedication to customer satisfaction.

480.

RingCentral has received numerous awards for its innovation, technology, and workplace culture.

481.

The company's acquisition of DeepAffects in 2021 brought AI-driven sentiment analysis and voice analytics to its platform.

482.

RingCentral's unified communication solutions help businesses streamline workflows and improve employee productivity.

483.

The company's focus on digital transformation aligns with the evolving nature of modern work environments.

484.

RingCentral's platform promotes collaboration among remote and distributed teams.

485.

The company's commitment to environmental sustainability includes efforts to reduce its carbon footprint.

486.

RingCentral's industry partnerships and integrations with leading platforms enhance its value proposition for customers.

487.

The company's earnings growth and financial performance have contributed to its status as a market leader.

488.

RingCentral's forward-looking approach involves continuous improvement and adaptation to emerging technologies.

489.

The company's cultural values prioritize teamwork, innovation, and a customer-centric mindset.

490.

RingCentral's solutions enable businesses to transition from legacy phone systems to modern cloud-based communication.

491.

The company's scalable services are suitable for businesses ranging from startups to enterprises.

492.

RingCentral's engagement with the developer community encourages the creation of third-party applications and integrations.

493.

The platform's admin controls allow businesses to customize communication settings and permissions.

494.

RingCentral's global data centers ensure reliable and secure communication services for users worldwide.

495.

The company's acquisition of MessageBird in 2021 further expanded its capabilities in customer engagement and communication channels.

496.

RingCentral's commitment to accessibility includes features for users with disabilities.

497.

The platform's flexibility allows businesses to integrate existing communication tools and workflows.

498.

RingCentral's "Engage Digital" solution enables businesses to manage interactions across various digital channels.

499.

The company's corporate social responsibility initiatives include community engagement and philanthropy.

500.

RingCentral's evolution from a virtual PBX system to a comprehensive communication and collaboration platform showcases its journey of innovation and growth.

501.

Aspendale is situated approximately 27 kilometers (17 miles) south-east of Melbourne's central business district.

502.

The suburb is part of the City of Kingston, which is known for its coastal lifestyle and natural beauty.

503.

Aspendale is bordered by Port Phillip Bay to the west, Mordialloc Creek to the north, and the suburbs of Edithvale and Aspendale Gardens to the south and east.

504.

The name "Aspendale" is thought to have originated from the Greek word "aspendos," which refers to a type of tree or plant.

505.

The area was initially used for market gardens and farming before urban development took place.

506.

Aspendale's beachfront location makes it a popular destination for swimming, fishing, and water activities.

507.

Aspendale Beach is known for its sandy shores, clear waters, and scenic views of the bay.

508.

The suburb is well-connected by transportation, with the Frankston railway line running through the area.

509.

Aspendale railway station provides convenient access to Melbourne's central business district and other parts of the city.

510.

The coastal trail along the beach is a favorite spot for walking, jogging, and cycling enthusiasts.

511.

One of the landmarks in Aspendale is the Aspendale Life Saving Club, which plays a vital role in beach safety and education.

512.

The neighboring suburbs of Aspendale Gardens and Edithvale offer additional amenities and recreational opportunities.

513.

Aspendale's residential areas are characterized by a mix of modern homes, older cottages, and apartments.

514.

The suburb's tree-lined streets and parks contribute to a relaxed and picturesque atmosphere.

515.

Residents can enjoy various local parks and reserves, including the Edithvale-Seaford Wetlands.

516.

The Aspendale Cricket Club and the Aspendale Tennis Club are active community organizations promoting sports and recreation.

517.

Aspendale Primary School serves the local community and has a history dating back to the late 1800s.

518.

The suburb is home to diverse dining options, from casual cafes to seafood restaurants.

519.

Aspendale's proximity to the beach provides opportunities for birdwatching and observing marine life.

520.

The scenic coastline offers stunning sunsets and a peaceful environment for relaxation.

521.

The suburb's coastal location also means that maritime activities, such as sailing and boating, are popular among residents.

522.

Aspendale's real estate market attracts those seeking a beachside lifestyle while remaining relatively close to the city.

523.

The nearby town of Chelsea offers additional shopping, dining, and entertainment options.

524.

The Aspendale Yacht Club is a hub for sailing enthusiasts and hosts various events and regattas.

525.

Aspendale's natural beauty and outdoor spaces make it a popular location for photography and artistic endeavors.

526.

The suburb's community spirit is evident through local events, markets, and gatherings.

527.

The Edithvale-Aspendale Sporting Club is a prominent venue for Australian rules football and cricket.

528.

Aspendale's beach is patrolled by lifeguards during peak times, ensuring the safety of beachgoers.

529.

The area's coastal vegetation and sand dunes play a vital role in preserving the local ecosystem.

530.

The suburb's access to public transportation and major roadways contributes to its connectivity with neighboring areas.

531.

Aspendale's relaxed and family-friendly atmosphere makes it an attractive place to raise children.

532.

The proximity to shopping centers and essential services adds to the convenience of living in Aspendale.

533.

The suburb's history is reflected in its mix of architectural styles, ranging from period homes to modern designs.

534.

The Aspendale Gardens Shopping Centre provides retail and dining options to residents.

535.

Aspendale is known for its community events, including festivals, markets, and outdoor concerts.

536.

The Aspendale Historical Society contributes to preserving and sharing the area's heritage.

537.

The suburb's seaside location has inspired many artists and writers throughout the years.

538.

The Aspendale Railway Station features a mural that depicts the area's history and natural beauty.

539.

Aspendale's coastal charm makes it a popular spot for weddings, photography sessions, and special occasions.

540.

The suburb's climate is influenced by its coastal position, resulting in mild temperatures and sea breezes.

541.

The Aspendale foreshore is a haven for birdwatchers, offering opportunities to spot native and migratory species.

542.

The Edithvale-Aspendale Little Athletics Club provides a nurturing environment for young athletes.

543.

Aspendale's schools and educational facilities contribute to the development of the local community.

544.

The suburb's community centers host workshops, classes, and social events for residents of all ages.

545.

The Aspendale Garden and Hardware store serves the local community's gardening and DIY needs.

546.

Aspendale's natural environment is home to a variety of flora and fauna, including coastal vegetation.

547.

The suburb's sense of community is enhanced by regular gatherings, such as beach clean-up events.

548.

Aspendale's coastal trails offer opportunities to explore the shoreline and discover hidden gems.

549.

The area's rich history and connection to the bay are celebrated through local art installations.

550.

Aspendale's blend of coastal living and suburban convenience makes it a sought-after destination for families, retirees, and those who appreciate a relaxed beachside lifestyle.

551.

The Jacob Broom House is named after its original owner, Jacob Broom, a signer of the United States Constitution.

552.

The house is an excellent example of Federal-style architecture, which was popular in the late 18th century.

553.

It was constructed in 1783, making it one of the oldest surviving buildings in Wilmington.

554.

The Jacob Broom House is located at 1313 Market Street in Wilmington's historic district.

555.

The house was built on a lot that Jacob Broom purchased in 1770, and it became his primary residence.

556.

Jacob Broom was born in 1752 and was a successful merchant and landowner in Delaware.

557.

Broom played a significant role in the American Revolution and later became involved in politics.

558.

He served in the Continental Congress and was one of the signers of
the United States Constitution in 1787.

559.

The house is a two-and-a-half-story brick structure with elegant
proportions and refined architectural details.

560.

The front façade of the house features a central entrance with a
fanlight and sidelights.

561.

The Jacob Broom House is renowned for its exceptional woodwork,
including delicate moldings and paneling.

562.

The interior of the house showcases period furnishings and
decorative elements, offering visitors a glimpse into the past.

563.

The house has been carefully restored and preserved, maintaining its
historical significance.

564.

In the 19th century, the house was used for various purposes,
including as a hotel and boarding house.

565.

It has survived various changes in the surrounding neighborhood and
witnessed the growth of Wilmington.

566.

The Jacob Broom House was added to the National Register of
Historic Places in 1971.

567.

Today, the house is operated as a museum by the Delaware Historical Society.

568.

Visitors to the museum can learn about Jacob Broom's life, the history of the Constitution, and the Federal period in America.

569.

The house offers guided tours that provide insights into the architectural details and historical context.

570.

The museum hosts educational programs, events, and exhibitions related to American history and culture.

571.

The Jacob Broom House is a designated National Historic Landmark, recognizing its importance in American history.

572.

The architecture of the house reflects the elegance and sophistication of the Federal style.

573.

The house's design features symmetry, classic proportions, and restrained ornamentation.

574.

The Jacob Broom House serves as a tangible link to the Founding Fathers and the creation of the United States.

575.

The house's location on Market Street places it in the heart of Wilmington's historic district.

576.

The museum contributes to the cultural enrichment of the local community and attracts visitors interested in history and architecture.

577.

The restoration of the house aimed to maintain its authenticity and preserve its historical integrity.

578.

The Jacob Broom House provides visitors with a glimpse into the daily life of an important figure from the Revolutionary era.

579.

The house's furnishings and décor are carefully curated to reflect the style of the late 18th century.

580.

The museum offers a unique opportunity to explore Delaware's role in the formation of the nation.

581.

The Jacob Broom House is an important educational resource for students, scholars, and history enthusiasts.

582.

The museum's exhibits showcase artifacts, documents, and memorabilia related to Jacob Broom's life and times.

583.

The house's architecture and historical significance make it a valuable asset to Wilmington's cultural heritage.

584.

The Jacob Broom House serves as a reminder of the values and ideals that shaped the United States.

585.

Visitors can experience the ambiance of the late 1700s while exploring the house's rooms and chambers.

586.

The house's restoration efforts were guided by historical research and a commitment to preserving authenticity.

587.

The museum offers interactive exhibits that engage visitors of all ages in learning about American history.

588.

The Jacob Broom House is an example of adaptive reuse, as it has served different purposes over the centuries.

589.

The museum's staff and volunteers work diligently to provide informative and engaging tours to visitors.

590.

The house's location on Market Street makes it easily accessible for tourists and locals alike.

591.

The Jacob Broom House contributes to the cultural tourism industry in Wilmington and Delaware.

592.

The museum's exhibits highlight the challenges and debates that shaped the creation of the U.S. Constitution.

593.

The Federal-style architecture of the house reflects the neoclassical influences of the late 18th century.

594.

The museum's programs foster a greater understanding of Delaware's contributions to American history.

595.

The Jacob Broom House exemplifies the historical importance of preserving architectural heritage.

596.

The house's connection to Jacob Broom's legacy adds depth to its historical narrative.

597.

The museum's exhibits explore the social, political, and economic contexts of the late 1700s.

598.

The Jacob Broom House offers a serene and reflective space where visitors can connect with the past.

599.

The museum's educational initiatives extend beyond its walls, reaching students and schools across Delaware.

600.

The Jacob Broom House stands as a testament to the enduring
significance of the Founding Fathers' ideals and contributions to the
United States.

601.

The Italian Wolf (Canis lupus italicus) is a subspecies of the gray
wolf native to Italy and the surrounding regions.

602.

It's one of the smallest subspecies of gray wolves, with males
weighing around 55-77 pounds and females around 44-66 pounds.

603.

The Italian Wolf has a distinctive reddish-brown coat with dark
markings and a pale underside.

604.

This wolf subspecies has adapted to a variety of habitats, including
mountains, forests, and grasslands.

605.

Historically, the Italian Wolf's range extended beyond Italy,
including parts of France and the Balkans.

606.

The population of Italian Wolves sharply declined due to habitat loss
and human persecution over the centuries.

607.

The Italian Wolf was classified as an endangered species in Italy in
the 1970s.

608.

Efforts to protect and conserve the Italian Wolf began in the 1980s, including habitat restoration and legal protections.

609.

The Italian Wolf is an apex predator, helping to maintain a balance in the ecosystem by controlling herbivore populations.

610.

They primarily hunt small to medium-sized ungulates like roe deer, chamois, and wild boar.

611.

The Italian Wolf also feeds on smaller prey like rabbits, hares, and rodents.

612.

The wolf's social structure consists of a pack led by an alpha pair, which is typically the breeding pair.

613.

Italian Wolves communicate through various vocalizations, including howls, barks, and growls.

614.

Their howling serves as a way to mark territory and communicate with other packs.

615.

Breeding season for Italian Wolves usually occurs between January and March.

616.

The alpha female gives birth to a litter of 3 to 6 pups after a gestation period of around 63 days.

617.

The entire pack contributes to raising and caring for the pups, which are born blind and helpless.

618.

Italian Wolves play a crucial role in the natural balance of ecosystems by regulating herbivore populations.

619.

They help prevent overgrazing of vegetation by controlling deer and other prey populations.

620.

Conservation efforts for the Italian Wolf include habitat preservation, reintroduction programs, and public awareness campaigns.

621.

The Italian Wolf is a protected species in Italy and the European Union.

622.

Wolf-human conflicts sometimes arise due to livestock predation, leading to ongoing discussions about coexistence strategies.

623.

In Italy, the wolf has cultural significance and is depicted in various historical artifacts and art.

624.

The Italian Wolf's distinct howling can be heard echoing through the Apennine Mountains.

625.

The Italian Wolf is known by different names in various languages, such as "Lupo Italiano" in Italian and "Loup d'Italie" in French.

626.

The subspecies is closely related to other Eurasian wolf populations.

627.

Genetic studies have helped researchers understand the unique characteristics and origins of the Italian Wolf.

628.

The Italian Wolf is recognized as a symbol of biodiversity and wilderness conservation in Italy.

629.

Conservation organizations work to mitigate human-wolf conflicts and promote understanding among local communities.

630.

The reintroduction of the Italian Wolf in certain regions has shown positive effects on local ecosystems.

631.

The wolf's presence has been associated with increased biodiversity and improved forest health.

632.

The Italian Wolf's role as a top predator helps maintain the balance of the food chain.

633.

Wolf tourism has emerged in some regions, offering educational opportunities for visitors to learn about and appreciate these animals.

634.

The Italian Wolf's survival is closely tied to the protection of its habitat and the availability of natural prey.

635.

Camera traps and tracking collars are used to monitor the behavior and movement of Italian Wolf populations.

636.

Conservationists collaborate with local communities to develop strategies that minimize conflicts between wolves and humans.

637.

The Italian Wolf's recovery is a testament to the effectiveness of conservation efforts and community engagement.

638.

The subspecies has become a flagship species for broader conservation initiatives.

639.

The presence of wolves has also led to increased ecotourism, benefiting local economies.

640.

Scientific research on Italian Wolves contributes to our understanding of wolf behavior, ecology, and conservation.

641.

The Italian Wolf's ability to thrive in human-altered landscapes demonstrates its adaptability.

642.

Wolves have been integral to myths, legends, and cultural narratives in various societies for centuries.

643.

Conservation organizations collaborate internationally to share knowledge and best practices for wolf recovery.

644.

The Italian Wolf is part of a broader network of wolf populations across Europe and Asia.

645.

Wolves play a vital role in maintaining the health and vitality of ecosystems by controlling prey populations.

646.

The recovery of the Italian Wolf serves as a symbol of successful species restoration efforts.

647.

The species' revival has sparked conversations about the importance of preserving biodiversity.

648.

The Italian Wolf's resurgence highlights the potential for human-wildlife coexistence and ecosystem restoration.

649.

In 2007, the Italian government declared May 2nd as "Italian Wolf Day" to raise awareness about wolf conservation.

650.

The Italian Wolf's story is a testament to the resilience of nature and the impact of collaborative conservation efforts.

651.

Jackals are medium-sized carnivores that belong to the Canidae family, which includes wolves, foxes, and domestic dogs.

652.

There are three main species of jackals: the golden jackal, the black-backed jackal, and the side-striped jackal.

653.

Jackals are found in various regions across Africa, Asia, and southeastern Europe.

654.

The golden jackal is the most widely distributed and adaptable among the jackal species.

655.

Jackals are known for their distinct vocalizations, which include howls, yelps, and barks. These calls help them communicate with other members of their group.

656.

They often form monogamous pairs and live in small family groups.

657.

Jackals are opportunistic omnivores, meaning they eat a variety of food including small mammals, birds, insects, fruits, and carrion.

658.

Their keen sense of smell helps them locate food, even buried beneath the ground.

659.

Jackals are known for their ability to scavenge and take advantage of food resources left behind by other predators.

660.

The black-backed jackal's diet is quite diverse, including rodents, insects, fruits, and occasionally larger prey like antelope fawns.

661.

Side-striped jackals have a more frugivorous diet, with a focus on eating fruits and insects.

662.

Jackals are well adapted for both hunting and scavenging, with a lean body and strong legs for running.

663.

The golden jackal has a versatile diet and can thrive in various habitats, including grasslands, forests, and urban areas.

664.

Jackals play a role in controlling rodent populations, helping to keep ecosystem balances in check.

665.

Jackals have a keen sense of hearing and sight, which aids them in detecting potential threats and prey.

666.

They are known to be shy and elusive animals, often avoiding interactions with larger predators.

667.

Jackals have well-developed social behaviors and often exhibit cooperative hunting and pack activities.

668.

Their fur can vary in color from pale gold to reddish-brown, with lighter undersides.

669.

Jackals are territorial and use scent marking and vocalizations to establish and defend their territories.

670.

Their communication through howling is used to indicate territory boundaries and attract potential mates.

671.

Jackals are known for their strong family bonds, often helping to care for the young in their pack.

672.

Mating pairs often engage in mutual grooming as a way to strengthen their bond.

673.

Jackal pups are born blind and dependent on their parents for care and protection.

674.

Pups begin to eat solid food after a few weeks but remain with their parents for several months before becoming independent.

675.

Jackals are sometimes considered pests by humans due to their scavenging habits and potential for livestock predation.

676.

In certain cultures and myths, jackals are depicted as cunning and clever animals.

677.

Jackals have been a subject of folklore and symbolism in various cultures, representing both positive and negative traits.

678.

Jackals are often associated with the nighttime and are sometimes seen as symbols of transformation or cunning.

679.

The ancient Egyptians believed that the god Anubis, associated with mummification and the afterlife, had the head of a jackal.

680.

In parts of Africa, jackals are considered sacred animals and are associated with spiritual beliefs.

681.

The hyena is sometimes confused with jackals due to their similar scavenging habits, but they belong to different genera.

682.

The side-striped jackal is named after its distinctive stripe pattern along its sides.

683.

The golden jackal's scientific name is Canis aureus, derived from the Latin words for "dog" and "gold."

684.

Jackals have a life span of around 10-15 years in the wild.

685.

The side-striped jackal is known for its solitary behavior compared to other jackal species.

686.

Black-backed jackals are often found in grasslands, savannas, and woodland areas.

687.

Golden jackals have a more varied habitat range, including deserts, marshes, and urban areas.

688.

The African golden wolf was recently reclassified as a separate species, distinct from the golden jackal.

689.

Jackals have adapted to changing landscapes and habitats, even living near human settlements and farmlands.

690.

Urbanization has led to increased interactions between jackals and humans.

691.

Jackals are sometimes hunted for their fur, although hunting them is regulated in many areas.

692.

Conservation efforts vary for different jackal species, with some populations facing habitat loss and human conflicts.

693.

Jackals play a crucial role in maintaining the ecological balance of their habitats.

694.

Some jackal species have been negatively impacted by habitat fragmentation and human activity.

695.

In India, the golden jackal is known for its adaptability to various environments, from forests to urban areas.

696.

Jackals are considered part of the natural ecosystems in which they reside, influencing prey populations and helping to control disease vectors.

697.

The IUCN Red List classifies some jackal species as "Least Concern" due to their relatively stable populations, while others are classified as "Near Threatened" or "Vulnerable."

698.

Conservation efforts often focus on understanding jackal behavior and ecology to better manage and protect their populations.

699.

Jackals are key indicators of ecosystem health and can serve as "umbrella species" for broader conservation efforts.

700.

Jackals remain a symbol of adaptability and survival in a changing world, embodying the complex relationships between wildlife, humans, and their shared environments.

701.

Zappos was founded in 1999 by Nick Swinmurn, who struggled to find a specific pair of shoes in his size at a local mall.

702.

The company's original name was "ShoeSite.com," which was later changed to "Zappos," a play on the Spanish word "zapatos," meaning shoes.

703.

Zappos officially launched its website in June 1999, initially focusing exclusively on shoe sales.

704.

The company's first headquarters was a small apartment in San Francisco.

705.

Tony Hsieh, a venture capitalist, joined Zappos as an investor and eventually became its CEO in 2000.

706.

Zappos struggled financially during its early years, with reports of employees having to haul in shelves to keep the company's servers from being confiscated due to unpaid bills.

707.

In 2003, Zappos moved its headquarters to Henderson, Nevada, and expanded its product offerings to include clothing, accessories, and more.

708.

One of Zappos' key strategies was its commitment to exceptional customer service, famously aiming to "deliver happiness."

709.

Zappos differentiated itself by offering free shipping and returns, even on products that customers didn't end up keeping.

710.

The company implemented a unique call center model, allowing customer service representatives to spend as much time on calls as needed to satisfy customers.

711.

Zappos also developed a 365-day return policy, giving customers a full year to return products for a refund.

712.

By 2009, Zappos was generating over $1 billion in annual gross merchandise sales.

713.

Amazon announced its acquisition of Zappos in July 2009 in a deal valued at approximately $1.2 billion.

714.

Despite the acquisition, Zappos continued to operate as an independent subsidiary under the Amazon umbrella.

715.

Zappos maintained its distinct company culture, which included unique office designs, a focus on employee happiness, and a relaxed dress code.

716.

The company's core values, including "Deliver WOW through service" and "Create fun and a little weirdness," helped shape its corporate identity.

717.

Zappos' corporate culture and practices attracted significant attention, leading to books like "Delivering Happiness" authored by Tony Hsieh.

718.

Zappos introduced the "Holacracy" organizational structure, aiming to empower employees to make decisions and drive innovation.

719.

In 2013, Zappos eliminated traditional job titles and embraced a self-management approach through Holacracy.

720.

The company was known for its innovative and playful office spaces, including a slide connecting two floors and a "monkey room" for creative brainstorming.

721.

Zappos celebrated its 10th anniversary in 2009 by offering free shoes to all Facebook fans.

722.

Zappos launched the Zappos Adaptive program to provide shoes and clothing for people with disabilities.

723.

The company introduced Zappos Couture, a high-end fashion platform featuring luxury brands.

724.

Zappos initiated the "Friends With Benefits" loyalty program, offering free expedited shipping and rewards to frequent customers.

725.

The Zappos for Good initiative focused on giving back to the community through volunteering, charitable donations, and social impact programs.

726.

Zappos' "Customer Loyalty Team" was renowned for their exceptional dedication to customer satisfaction.

727.

The company occasionally surprised and delighted customers by upgrading their shipping to overnight delivery for no extra charge.

728.

In 2011, Zappos experienced a security breach, prompting a temporary shutdown of its site to protect customer data.

729.

The company took a creative approach to marketing, organizing events like the "Zappos.com Rock 'n' Roll Marathon Series."

730.

Zappos' unique company culture led to its inclusion on numerous "Best Places to Work" lists over the years.

731.

Tony Hsieh authored the book "Delivering Happiness," sharing insights into Zappos' customer-centric philosophy and employee culture.

732.

In 2015, Zappos introduced the "Zappos Insights" program, offering workshops and consulting to share its organizational practices.

733.

Zappos celebrated its 20th anniversary in 2019, reflecting on its journey and continued commitment to customer satisfaction.

734.

Tragically, Tony Hsieh passed away in November 2020, leaving behind a legacy of innovation and customer-focused business practices.

735.

Under Hsieh's leadership, Zappos' company culture was driven by values like authenticity, open communication, and embracing individuality.

736.

Zappos continued to prioritize employee well-being, offering benefits like free life coaching and mental health support.

737.

In 2021, Zappos officially retired its Holacracy structure, reverting to a more traditional organizational model.

738.

The company maintained its commitment to customer service and unique culture despite changes in leadership and organizational structure.

739.

Over the years, Zappos expanded its product range to include a wide variety of footwear, clothing, accessories, and more.

740.

Zappos' dedication to customer service often resulted in memorable customer interactions and stories shared online.

741.

The company's playful and unconventional marketing campaigns included initiatives like the "Zappos Family Album," featuring employees and customers.

742.

Zappos occasionally hosted customer events like "Zappos Insights Live," providing opportunities for learning and networking.

743.

The company's focus on community and employee engagement remained evident through events like the annual "Zappos All Hands" gathering.

744.

Zappos was known for its commitment to sustainability, recycling shoes, and participating in eco-friendly initiatives.

745.

The company leveraged social media platforms to engage with customers and share its values and culture.

746.

Zappos' website featured a variety of interactive elements, such as customer reviews, videos, and detailed product descriptions.

747.

The company's commitment to transparent communication extended to sharing its story, challenges, and lessons learned.

748.

Zappos' philanthropic efforts included initiatives like "Zappos for Good" and partnerships with charitable organizations.

749.

The company's commitment to exceptional service earned it a loyal customer base and positive word-of-mouth marketing.

750.

Zappos' journey from its humble beginnings to its acquisition by Amazon and its impact on e-commerce and company culture showcases its enduring legacy in the business world.

751.

Lenovo was founded on November 1, 1984, in Beijing, China, by a group of 11 engineers led by Liu Chuanzhi.

752.

Originally named "Legend," the company initially focused on distributing technology products, including imported computers.

753.

In 1988, Legend introduced its first computer, the Legend PC, which was inspired by the IBM PC.

754.

By the early 1990s, Lenovo had become a leading computer manufacturer in China, specializing in desktop computers.

755.

The company's name was changed to Lenovo in 2003 to accommodate its global expansion plans.

756.

Lenovo's acquisition of IBM's Personal Computing Division in 2005 marked a significant milestone, making it a global player in the PC market.

757.

The acquisition included the iconic ThinkPad line of laptops, which became synonymous with durability and innovation.

758.

Lenovo's acquisition of IBM's PC business was one of the largest cross-border acquisitions by a Chinese company at that time.

759.

Lenovo's international headquarters is in Morrisville, North Carolina, while its operational headquarters is in Beijing.

760.

Yang Yuanqing, who joined Lenovo in 1989, became its Chairman and CEO in 2009.

761.

Lenovo's "Protect and Attack" strategy focuses on maintaining its position in the PC market while expanding into new areas, like smartphones and data centers.

762.

In 2013, Lenovo acquired Motorola Mobility from Google, giving it a foothold in the smartphone industry.

763.

Lenovo's Yoga line of laptops, introduced in 2012, gained attention for their flexible hinges that allowed them to function as laptops or tablets.

764.

The ThinkPad X1 Carbon, launched in 2012, became one of Lenovo's flagship laptops, known for its lightweight design and durability.

765.

Lenovo's innovation center, the Lenovo Research Center, is responsible for developing cutting-edge technology, such as foldable screens and VR/AR solutions.

766.

In 2016, Lenovo unveiled the first commercial smartphone with Google's Project Tango technology, offering augmented reality capabilities.

767.

The company's data center solutions division focuses on developing servers, storage systems, and networking products.

768.

Lenovo has consistently ranked among the world's top PC manufacturers, competing with companies like HP and Dell.

769.

In 2017, Lenovo celebrated the 25th anniversary of the ThinkPad laptop with the release of the retro-styled ThinkPad 25.

770.

Lenovo's commitment to sustainability includes efforts to reduce its carbon footprint, improve energy efficiency, and promote recycling.

771.

The company launched its first 5G laptop, the Lenovo Flex 5G, in 2020, leveraging the capabilities of next-generation cellular networks.

772.

Lenovo is known for its commitment to diversity and inclusion, with various initiatives aimed at promoting equality within the company.

773.

In 2020, Lenovo introduced the ThinkPad X1 Fold, the world's first foldable PC with a flexible OLED screen.

774.

The company's focus on smart devices includes products like smart displays, tablets, and smart home technology.

775.

Lenovo has a strong presence in the education sector, providing technology solutions and devices for classrooms.

776.

The company's gaming division, Legion, produces high-performance laptops, desktops, and accessories for gamers.

777.

Lenovo's annual Tech World Innovation Summit showcases its latest innovations and technology advancements.

778.

The Lenovo Foundation focuses on charitable initiatives, including supporting education, disaster relief, and community development.

779.

In 2021, Lenovo launched its first AR glasses, the Lenovo ThinkReality A3, designed for enterprise and industrial use.

780.

Lenovo's joint venture with Fujitsu created the company Fujitsu Client Computing Limited, strengthening its presence in Japan.

781.

The company's 360-degree rotation laptops, like the Yoga series, have earned praise for their versatility and functionality.

782.

Lenovo consistently invests in research and development, striving to be at the forefront of technological advancements.

783.

The "Three-wave Strategy" outlines Lenovo's approach to focusing on core businesses, growth businesses, and new businesses.

784.

The company has faced challenges related to cybersecurity and data privacy, prompting efforts to enhance security measures.

785.

Lenovo's workforce comprises employees from diverse backgrounds and nationalities, reflecting its global footprint.

786.

The company's cultural transformation has been driven by its "We are Lenovo" initiative, emphasizing collaboration and innovation.

787.

Lenovo's commitment to sustainability includes setting ambitious carbon reduction targets and promoting a circular economy.

788.

The company operates in over 180 countries, with a strong global distribution network.

789.

Lenovo's brand values include "Customer Obsession," "Results-Driven," "Innovation," and "Integrity."

790.

The ThinkBook series, launched in 2019, targets small and medium-sized businesses with a focus on modern design and productivity.

791.

Lenovo's services division offers a range of solutions, including device management, support, and warranty services.

792.

The company's global headquarters in Beijing, known as the "Lenovo Building," showcases innovative architecture and sustainable design.

793.

Lenovo's innovation centers around the world facilitate collaboration with partners, startups, and customers.

794.

The company has consistently ranked in the Fortune Global 500 list of the world's largest corporations.

795.

Lenovo's philanthropic efforts extend to disaster relief, education initiatives, and support for underserved communities.

796.

The company's laptops, particularly those in the ThinkPad line, are often praised for their keyboards and durability.

797.

Lenovo's leadership team includes professionals with diverse expertise in technology, business, and innovation.

798.

The company has made strides in AI and machine learning, incorporating these technologies into its products and services.

799.

Lenovo's Vision and Mission statement focuses on enabling smarter technology for all and driving customer success.

800.

The history of Lenovo is a testament to its evolution from a Chinese startup to a global technology powerhouse, influencing various industries and pioneering innovative solutions.

801.

The Corbit-Sharp House is located in Odessa, Delaware, and is a National Historic Landmark.

802.

It was built in 1774 by William Corbit, a prosperous Quaker merchant, and is considered one of the finest examples of Georgian architecture in the United States.

803.

The house is named after its original owner, William Corbit, and later owner, Judge James P. Sharp.

804.

The Corbit-Sharp House is renowned for its exceptional preservation and period accuracy.

805.

The house has a central hallway plan with symmetrical rooms on either side, typical of Georgian architecture.

806.

The building's exterior features red brick construction and elegant detailing, such as keystones and a dentil cornice.

807.

The Corbit-Sharp House has a gambrel roof, a characteristic feature of Dutch Colonial architecture.

808.

The house has a historic garden that replicates the colonial-era garden design, complete with heirloom plants.

809.

It serves as a museum today, showcasing both the house's history and the lifestyle of the 18th-century inhabitants.

810.

The house contains original furniture, including pieces owned by the Corbit and Sharp families.

811.

The Corbit-Sharp House offers guided tours that provide insights into daily life during the colonial period.

812.

The house has been featured in architectural and historical publications for its significance.

813.

It is part of the Historic Odessa Foundation, which works to preserve and interpret the history of the region.

814.

The Corbit-Sharp House's interior is adorned with period-appropriate wallpapers, textiles, and decorations.

815.

The house's woodwork, including paneling and moldings, reflects the craftsmanship of the time.

816.

The formal parlor of the house features a prominent corner fireplace, a focal point of the room.

817.

The house's dining room is set with a table and chairs, showcasing how meals were served during the 18th century.

818.

Visitors to the Corbit-Sharp House can learn about the Quaker heritage of William Corbit and its influence on the architecture and lifestyle.

819.

The house offers educational programs and workshops for children and adults to learn about history and traditional crafts.

820.

The historic garden is meticulously maintained and features a variety of plants that were common during the colonial era.

821.

The house has a strong connection to the history of Delaware and its colonial past.

822.

It is often used as a backdrop for historical reenactments and events that celebrate the region's history.

823.

The Corbit-Sharp House showcases period-appropriate clothing and textiles, offering a glimpse into colonial fashion.

824.

The house's restoration and preservation efforts have earned recognition from historical preservation organizations.

825.

The property surrounding the house features authentic outbuildings, including a smokehouse and a privy.

826.

The Corbit-Sharp House serves as a hub for cultural and educational events within the community.

827.

The house's architecture and design reflect the colonial ideals of symmetry, proportion, and functionality.

828.

It provides insights into the daily life and customs of early American families, including their social and economic activities.

829.

The house's location in Odessa, Delaware, is an important historic town known for its well-preserved architecture.

830.

The Corbit-Sharp House's historical significance is linked to the broader history of Delaware and the United States during the colonial period.

831.

The house's period gardens are planted with heirloom varieties of vegetables, herbs, and flowers.

832.

The house's guided tours often include anecdotes and stories that provide a more personal connection to its former inhabitants.

833.

The Corbit-Sharp House offers a unique opportunity to step back in time and experience the 18th-century lifestyle.

834.

The house's furnishings and decorative arts offer a comprehensive look at the material culture of the time.

835.

The Corbit-Sharp House's architectural elements, such as its windows and doorways, showcase colonial craftsmanship.

836.

The house has been recognized by the National Park Service for its historical and architectural significance.

837.

It serves as a venue for special events, including weddings, receptions, and educational programs.

838.

The Corbit-Sharp House's preservation efforts extend to maintaining its structural integrity and original features.

839.

The house's interior includes rooms that were used for various purposes, such as sleeping quarters and a working kitchen.

840.

The house's collections include artifacts, documents, and textiles that shed light on the lives of the Corbit and Sharp families.

841.

The Corbit-Sharp House highlights the influence of European architectural styles on colonial American design.

842.

The house's well-preserved condition is a testament to the dedication of the Historic Odessa Foundation and its supporters.

843.

The property surrounding the house includes landscaped areas that complement the historic gardens.

844.

The Corbit-Sharp House's guided tours are led by knowledgeable docents who provide historical context and insights.

845.

The house's association with prominent individuals and families adds to its historical significance.

846.

The house's exterior features wooden shutters and a formal entrance, contributing to its architectural charm.

847.

The Corbit-Sharp House offers visitors a chance to explore the history of Delaware's colonial past and the people who lived there.

848.

It serves as a valuable educational resource for schools, allowing students to engage with history in a tangible way.

849.

The house's restoration efforts have focused on maintaining its authenticity while ensuring a comfortable experience for visitors.

850.

The Corbit-Sharp House stands as a testament to the importance of preserving historic structures and the stories they hold.

851.

The John Dickinson House is located in Dover, Delaware, and is a National Historic Landmark.

852.

The house was built in 1739 and served as the childhood home of John Dickinson, a Founding Father and key figure in American history.

853.

John Dickinson is often referred to as the "Penman of the Revolution" due to his influential writings advocating for American rights.

854.

The house is a fine example of Georgian architecture and features a symmetrical design and brick construction.

855.

It is one of the oldest surviving structures in Delaware and offers a glimpse into colonial life during the 18th century.

856.

The John Dickinson House showcases period-appropriate furnishings, providing visitors with an authentic experience of the era.

857.

The house's rooms are furnished with items that belonged to the Dickinson family, offering a tangible connection to history.

858.

John Dickinson's work included the "Letters from a Farmer in Pennsylvania," which argued against British taxation without representation.

859.

The house contains a library that holds books and documents relevant to John Dickinson's life and accomplishments.

860.

The John Dickinson House has been meticulously restored to its original appearance, preserving its historical integrity.

861.

The house's architecture reflects the influence of English architectural styles on colonial American design.

862.

Visitors can explore the house's gardens, which are landscaped to resemble the types of gardens common during the colonial period.

863.

The John Dickinson House is part of the First State National Historical Park, which encompasses several historic sites in Delaware.

864.

The house's historic interpretation and educational programs focus on John Dickinson's contributions to American independence.

865.

John Dickinson was a delegate to the Continental Congress and played a role in drafting the Articles of Confederation.

866.

The house's exhibits provide insights into John Dickinson's beliefs and how they influenced his writings.

867.

The John Dickinson House offers guided tours led by knowledgeable docents who share stories about the house and its occupants.

868.

The house's location in Dover, the capital of Delaware, adds to its historical significance within the state's history.

869.

The John Dickinson House's preservation efforts have been supported by various organizations and historical societies.

870.

The house's exterior features elements such as dormer windows, brick chimneys, and a central entrance.

871.

Visitors to the John Dickinson House can learn about colonial customs, social norms, and the role of the Dickinson family in society.

872.

The house's proximity to other historic sites and landmarks makes it a valuable stop for history enthusiasts.

873.

The John Dickinson House highlights the importance of individual contributions to the American Revolution.

874.

The property surrounding the house includes outbuildings that reflect the daily activities of colonial households.

875.

The house's architecture and design were influenced by the practical needs of the Dickinson family's daily life.

876.

The John Dickinson House is a place where visitors can learn about the challenges and debates leading up to the Revolutionary War.

877.

The house's interior includes period-appropriate wallpaper, furnishings, and decorative items.

878.

The John Dickinson House's collections include artifacts and documents that offer insights into the family's history.

879.

The house's historical interpretation emphasizes John Dickinson's role as a thinker, writer, and advocate for American rights.

880.

Visitors can explore the various rooms of the house, including the parlors, bedrooms, and dining areas.

881.

The John Dickinson House's architecture features Georgian-style proportions and details, showcasing craftsmanship of the time.

882.

The house's restoration involved extensive research to ensure that the furnishings and decor were historically accurate.

883.

The site offers educational programs for students, teachers, and the general public to learn about Delaware's colonial history.

884.

The John Dickinson House showcases the evolution of architectural styles and cultural influences in colonial America.

885.

The house is an example of how historical preservation can connect present generations with the ideals and struggles of the past.

886.

The John Dickinson House's interpretive exhibits highlight the interconnectedness of local history with national events.

887.

The house's gardens include plants that were commonly grown during the colonial period, offering a glimpse into early American horticulture.

888.

The John Dickinson House's location within a historic district contributes to its value as an educational and cultural resource.

889.

The house's historical significance extends beyond its physical structure, encompassing the ideas and values of John Dickinson.

890.

Visitors can gain a deeper understanding of John Dickinson's legacy as a statesman, writer, and supporter of American liberties.

891.

The house's preservation is a collaborative effort involving historians, preservationists, and community members.

892.

The John Dickinson House provides a window into the lifestyles, traditions, and aspirations of colonial Delawareans.

893.

The site's programming includes lectures, workshops, and special events that explore various aspects of colonial history.

894.

The house's location in Dover offers visitors the opportunity to explore other nearby historic sites and attractions.

895.

The John Dickinson House is a place where visitors can reflect on the intellectual and political climate of the 18th century.

896.

The house's exhibits present a balanced perspective on the complex issues and debates that shaped American history.

897.

The site's educational resources extend to digital platforms, allowing people to learn about John Dickinson's legacy online.

898.

The John Dickinson House is an important asset to the community, contributing to cultural enrichment and historical awareness.

899.

The house's architecture and design reflect the aspirations of early American settlers and their desire for a better future.

900.

The John Dickinson House serves as a tribute to the contributions of John Dickinson and his lasting impact on the nation's founding principles.

901.

Jaguars (Panthera onca) are large predatory big cats known for their strength and agility.

902.

Jaguars are native to the Americas and are primarily found in rainforests, swamps, and grasslands.

903.

Their range extends from the southern United States down to Argentina.

904.

Jaguars are solitary animals, preferring to hunt and live alone.

905.

They are primarily nocturnal, hunting during the night and resting during the day.

906.

Jaguars are strong swimmers and often hunt in water, including rivers and lakes.

907.

Their coat is usually tan or orange with distinctive black rosettes that serve as camouflage in their habitat.

908.

Some jaguars have a genetic mutation that results in a black coat, known as melanism, making them appear entirely black.

909.

Jaguars are the third-largest big cat species after tigers and lions.

910.

They have a robust build, with powerful jaws and strong teeth for hunting.

911.

Jaguars are apex predators, meaning they are at the top of the food chain in their ecosystem.

912.

Their strong limbs and sharp claws allow them to ambush and overpower their prey.

913.

Jaguars are opportunistic hunters and have a diverse diet, including deer, peccaries, monkeys, and fish.

914.

Jaguars mark their territory with scent markings and vocalizations to avoid encounters with other jaguars.

915.

Jaguars are classified as "Near Threatened" due to habitat loss and poaching.

916.

Jaguars hold cultural significance for many indigenous peoples in the Americas.

917.

Some indigenous cultures view jaguars as symbols of power, protection, and spiritual connection.

918.

Jaguars play a crucial role in maintaining the balance of their ecosystems by regulating prey populations.

919.

Jaguars have been observed interacting with other species like caimans and crocodiles, occasionally preying on them.

920.

Jaguars have one of the most powerful bites among big cats, enabling them to crush bones and skulls.

921.

Habitat fragmentation and conflict with humans are major threats to jaguars.

922.

Conservation organizations work to protect jaguar habitats and reduce human-jaguar conflicts.

923.

Jaguars primarily inhabit tropical rainforests, which are disappearing at an alarming rate.

924.

Jaguars have been revered in ancient civilizations, often representing strength and bravery.

925.

The jaguar holds significant symbolism in Mayan culture, representing power and rulership.

926.

The jaguar is the national animal of several Central and South American countries.

927.

Researchers use camera traps and tracking to learn more about jaguar behavior and movements.

928.

Jaguars communicate using various vocalizations, including roars and growls.

929.

Different subspecies of jaguars exist, with variations in coat patterns and sizes.

930.

Jaguars' adaptations vary based on their habitat, allowing them to thrive in different environments.

931.

Some zoos and wildlife parks participate in captive breeding programs to ensure the species' survival.

932.

Jaguars feature prominently in indigenous myths and legends across the Americas.

933.

Jaguars use a combination of stealth and brute force when hunting their prey.

934.

Their senses of sight, smell, and hearing are well-developed, aiding in hunting and survival.

935.

In the wild, jaguars typically live around 12-15 years, while those in captivity can live longer.

936.

Jaguars help control herbivore populations, preventing overgrazing and maintaining forest health.

937.

Jaguars are elusive and often avoid human contact, making them challenging to study in the wild.

938.

Jaguars have specially adapted paw pads that allow them to move silently through the forest.

939.

Establishing and maintaining protected areas is crucial for jaguar conservation.

940.

In different regions, jaguars are known by various names, such as "el tigre" in Spanish-speaking countries.

941.

In some areas, jaguars have been known to mate with other big cat species, resulting in hybrid offspring.

942.

Jaguars are often depicted as supernatural beings or deities in the myths of indigenous cultures.

943.

Eco-tourism focused on jaguar spotting can contribute to conservation efforts and local economies.

944.

Jaguars' physical prowess and fearlessness have contributed to their status as symbols of strength.

945.

Jaguars exhibit high levels of natural intelligence and adaptability in their hunting strategies.

946.

Jaguars often target prey that is easier to catch, optimizing energy expenditure.

947.

Jaguars can produce a sound similar to a domestic cat's purr, which is a communication method.

948.

As humans encroach on their habitat, conflicts between jaguars and livestock can arise.

949.

Jaguar motifs are found in indigenous art, pottery, and textiles across the Americas.

950.

Responsible wildlife tourism centered around jaguars can contribute to local economies and conservation efforts.

951.

The Jambu Fruit Dove (Ptilinopus jambu) is a beautifully colored bird found in Southeast Asia.

952.

Its name "jambu" is derived from the Malay word for rose apple, which is a fruit it commonly feeds on.

953.

These doves are known for their striking appearance, with males displaying vibrant plumage of deep pink, purple, and green, while females exhibit more subdued green colors.

954.

Jambu Fruit Doves primarily inhabit lowland rainforests and montane forests in countries like Malaysia, Indonesia, and Thailand.

955.

These birds play an important role in seed dispersal for various plant species by consuming fruits and then distributing the seeds through their droppings.

956.

Despite their vibrant colors, Jambu Fruit Doves are incredibly elusive and difficult to spot due to their habit of staying high up in the forest canopy.

957.

They have a distinctive call, which is often described as a soft cooing sound.

958.

Jambu Fruit Doves have a preference for small, fleshy fruits, and their diet can include a variety of berries and figs in addition to rose apples.

959.

Males use their vibrant plumage to attract females during courtship displays, which involve fluttering and bowing movements.

960.

These doves are known to exhibit strong territorial behavior, often defending their feeding and nesting areas from other males.

961.

Nests of Jambu Fruit Doves are usually built in the canopy of trees, where they construct flimsy platform-like structures from twigs and leaves.

962.

Female doves usually lay a single egg, which is incubated for around two weeks before hatching.

963.

Both parents take turns incubating the egg and caring for the chick after it hatches.

964.

Jambu Fruit Doves have a relatively short lifespan, usually living up to 5-6 years in the wild.

965.

They are considered to be a species of "Least Concern" according to the IUCN Red List, indicating that their population is relatively stable.

966.

The colors of the male Jambu Fruit Dove's plumage are believed to be a result of carotenoid pigments obtained from their diet.

967.

Deforestation and habitat loss are significant threats to the Jambu Fruit Dove population, as they rely on intact forests for their survival.

968.

These doves are sometimes kept in captivity as ornamental birds due to their vibrant colors.

969.

In Indonesia, the Jambu Fruit Dove is known as "Perkutut Jambu" and is often considered a symbol of beauty and grace.

970.

They are part of the larger family Columbidae, which includes all species of pigeons and doves.

971.

The Jambu Fruit Dove's scientific name, Ptilinopus jambu, combines the Greek word "ptilinopus" (meaning "plumage-loving") with "jambu" to reference its food preference.

972.

In Thai culture, the Jambu Fruit Dove is associated with the deity Nang Tani, a female ghost who is often depicted in the form of a beautiful woman sitting on a tree branch.

973.

Due to their shy nature, Jambu Fruit Doves are more often heard than seen, making their calls an integral part of the soundscape in their native habitats.

974.

These birds are known to forage alone or in pairs, rarely forming large flocks.

975.

They have a relatively slow flight and tend to move short distances between feeding sites.

976.

The Jambu Fruit Dove's wings produce a distinctive whistling sound during flight, which can help alert observers to their presence.

977.

Unlike many other bird species, Jambu Fruit Doves do not have a well-developed gizzard (muscular stomach) to grind down tough food items. Instead, they rely on their diet of soft fruits.

978.

The population density of these doves tends to be lower in areas where their preferred fruit sources are scarce.

979.

These doves are not known for their song but rather for their gentle cooing calls that are often heard echoing through the forest.

980.

Their coloring provides excellent camouflage within the dense foliage of their forest habitat.

981.

Some indigenous cultures in Southeast Asia have incorporated the Jambu Fruit Dove's feathers into their traditional clothing and accessories.

982.

The Jambu Fruit Dove is just one of many species of fruit doves that inhabit various regions around the world.

983.

The male Jambu Fruit Dove's bright colors are thought to play a role in attracting females, as these vibrant hues indicate good health and genetic fitness.

984.

These doves are important indicators of the health of their forest ecosystems. Their presence can reflect the availability of fruit-bearing plants and the overall ecological balance.

985.

The Jambu Fruit Dove's diet contributes to the dispersal of fruiting plants, aiding in the continuation of the forest ecosystem.

986.

While their main diet consists of fruit, they have been observed consuming small insects occasionally, possibly for added nutrients.

987.

In captivity, Jambu Fruit Doves require a diet that closely mimics their natural feeding habits, including a variety of soft fruits.

988.

Their unique colors have also made them a target for illegal wildlife trade, further endangering their populations in the wild.

989.

Jambu Fruit Doves are not known for their strong migratory tendencies, preferring to remain within their forest habitats.

990.

Some subspecies of Jambu Fruit Dove exhibit slight variations in their plumage colors, adding to the overall diversity of the species.

991.

These doves are admired by birdwatchers and nature enthusiasts for their rarity and elusive nature.

992.

The Jambu Fruit Dove's role in seed dispersal contributes to the maintenance of plant diversity and the regeneration of forests.

993.

Due to their reliance on specific forest types, changes in habitat structure and composition can impact their ability to find suitable food sources and nesting sites.

994.

Conservation efforts aimed at protecting the Jambu Fruit Dove's habitat can have positive effects on the overall health of their ecosystems.

995.

The populations of Jambu Fruit Doves can experience fluctuations based on the availability of fruiting trees and other environmental factors.

996.

Their distinct appearance has made them a popular subject for bird artists and illustrators.

997.

Climate change can potentially impact the distribution and availability of suitable habitats for these doves.

998.

Local folklore and traditions in their native regions often include stories and beliefs associated with the Jambu Fruit Dove.

999.

Some conservation organizations work to raise awareness about the importance of protecting the Jambu Fruit Dove and its habitat.

1000.

Observing and studying the behavior of Jambu Fruit Doves provides valuable insights into the intricate interactions between birds, plants, and their environment in tropical rainforests.